# For Government: Toward a Christian View of Authority

eicc
publications

Published by EICC Publications, a ministry of the Ezra Institute for Contemporary Christianity, PO Box 9, Stn. Main, Grimsby, ON L3M 1M0

Unless otherwise noted, Scripture quotations are taken from the Holman Christian Standard Bible (HCSB)

For volume pricing please contact the Ezra Institute for Contemporary Christianity: info@ezrainstitute.ca.

For Government: Toward a Christian View of Authority
ISBN: 978-1-989169-12-4

# For Government: Toward a Christian View of Authority

**CONTENTS**

# Religion, Government and the Secularist Illusion

## YOU GOTTA SERVE SOMEBODY

This small book on a Christian view of government begins, I think necessarily, with a brief consideration of the nature and meaning of religion. If that makes us narrow our eyes, it's probably because we have been conditioned to think for two or three generations that religion is something belonging to a private arena of life that can have no decisive bearing on the public space. Even if you live in a country where church and state are not *formally* separated (the United Kingdom for example), modern Western governments still operate on the assumption of an implicit separation between the 'personal faith' of politicians and civil administrators and the values, mission and responsibilities of government.

Moreover, we have been deeply steeped in a reductionistic understanding of government that presumes the use of the definite article. We speak of "*the* government" as though the administrators of civil life were the only ones involved in the business of governing – yet this truncation of government also has a religious character. The biblical worldview acknowledges the public legal order as just one of *several* legitimate, God-ordained spheres of authority (that is, governance), all of which are created to function in subjection to the authority of Jesus, the King of kings. So I begin this discussion reflecting on the nature and role of religion because, fundamentally, I believe the operative presupposition of a separation of faith and government, of religion and the public space is an impossible myth. It is a lie, used to push the Christian faith out of sight and mind, replacing it with a new religious order.

The question of government is in reality a question of true or false worship. In the words of that modern minstrel Bob Dylan, you gotta serve somebody…

## THE NEED TO EXPLAIN

Upon serious reflection it is evident that there is an unbreakable link between our concept of God (a divine or unconditioned reality), our view of ourselves, and how we choose to live in the world. Which is to say, what we *believe* shapes how we *behave* – our ideas have real- world consequences. This is because, from a scriptural standpoint, human beings are integral creatures and religious by nature. By integral I mean *first* that humankind is not formed of two or more alien substances, temporarily bound together (like soul substance and material substance as many ancient Greeks held) in an uncomfortable union, but are made *whole* as God's image-bearers and find that all the various aspects of our lives and experience come together in a concentration point we often call the heart, or soul – the inner person or religious root of our being (2 Cor. 4:16; 1 Pt. 3:4).

*Second*, it is in this heart that we long for *harmony* between the various aspects of life – we seek an integral life. Ordinarily we dislike contradiction and confusion. If we truly believe something and are committed to it, we typically want that fact to shape our thinking and living. We generally seek to avoid blatant inconsistency. We abhor hypocrisy (especially in others) and are driven by a desire for unity and integrity in our lives that results in a sense of overall purpose and meaning. In other words, we are wired to seek to *integrate* the various aspects of our lives into a coherent whole. If we don't do this our lives start to fall apart – to *disintegrate*.

We are also *religious* beings. This, I suggest, is an inescapable aspect of the human condition (Acts 17:22-23; Rom 1:18-25). There have been many attempts to explain human religious sensibility. Modernist philosophers have tried to account for the hardwired religious inclination of humanity in terms of the contrast between man and the magnitude of the cosmos he inhabits – a shoreless universe inspiring him with awe and fear. The various 'religions,' they claim, developed as a *defense mechanism* in which many unseen forces were posited, deified, sometimes anthropomorphized, and then ritually placated as a way of trying to gain some kind of control in a dangerous world, despite a sense of powerlessness. This is a typically secular and simplistic account of religion that implies modern technological man has outgrown such things; modern man now offers scientific explanations for various phenomena instead.

While there is an element of truth in seeing certain pagan religious practices as a form of defense mechanism, the ongoing prevalence of all kinds of superstitious beliefs about the world in our own culture undermines secular simplistic explanations. Just consider the West's huge contemporary interest in pagan religion, mythology and witchcraft, as well as the ubiquity of occultism, alternative medicine, spiritism, and astrology, and the incredible popularity of Eastern religions like Buddhism, Hinduism, and what was dubbed in the 1970s the New Age (a term no longer used because it is now mainstream). The idea that our era has outgrown various divinity beliefs and concepts in the wake of the scientific revolution, or that empirical science has essentially dispensed with various 'spiritual' perspectives on the world is patently false. Humans are religious beings who cannot help but seek to refer themselves back to the origin of all things.

## LIFE IS RELIGION

It is admittedly notoriously difficult to define *religion* to the satisfaction of everyone. The Latin words *religio* and *religare* probably take us to its root meanings of "reverence" (*religio*), and "to tie, to bind" (*religare*). The core idea here is a basic and fundamental tie that binds people together to get them growing in the same direction – an agricultural metaphor. Put another way, religion concerns the spiritual *root* of existence constituting the *ground of unity* for human life and society.

When thinking about religious awareness from a biblical standpoint we find that human beings somehow *transcend* the world in which we exist, living as what C.S. Lewis memorably referred to as a sort of spiritual amphibian. Though we are certainly created for this world (Gen. 1-2), living as dependent creatures in temporal reality, we are clearly made for fellowship with the eternal God, and so we find that eternity is in our hearts (Eccl. 3:11). It is for this reason St. Augustine famously prayed to God, "*You have made us for yourself and our hearts are restless until they find their rest in thee.*"[1] So, from a Christian perspective, human beings, who alone of all creatures can rationally reflect on their condition, are essentially and inescapably *religious beings* because of the relationship we each sustain to God our creator and the ineradicable sense we carry of our dependency and accountability.

Religion is therefore much more than the *practice* of this or that set of rituals. Religion is an all-encompassing reality that may or may not be connected to cultic rites and liturgy – in fact most religious perspectives are not. The philosopher Herman Dooyeweerd argues that the faith function of people's lives, which is subject to God's revelation as the *norm* for faith,

> …issues from the religious root of our temporal life, namely the heart, soul, or spirit of a person. Because of the fall into sin, the hearts of human beings turned away from God and the religious ground-motive of apostasy took hold of their faith and of their whole temporal life. Only the Spirit of God causes the rebirth of our hearts in Christ and radically reverses the direction of our temporal function of faith.[2]

Yet no matter how far it has fallen from the truth, "faith is always oriented to divine revelation,"[3] the only question is *how* people will respond. Thus, from the biblical standpoint, *all of life is religion* as we either worship and serve the living God in all aspects of life, or, because of our fallen condition, are turned toward the worship of aspects of creation (Romans 1); the honor of surrogate gods, which Scripture calls idolatry.

This idolatry may well take on an *ideological character* where one or more aspects of creation are identified, and then absolutized as being the root of all meaning and foundation of all explanations. For example, in ideologies like *communism* the community is absolutized; in *rationalism* the logical aspect or mind; in *individualism* the individual; in *romanticism* the emotional aspect; in *economism* the economical aspect of creation; in *materialism* the physical aspect; in *evolutionism*, the biotic, and so forth. The many *ism's* in Western cultural thought are the surrogate gods of the modern world.

In its broadest sense then, religion is *man's answer* to God's Word revelation; it is our varied human response as creatures to our creator. Every mother's son of us does give an answer whether we realize it or not. Again, it is not a matter of whether, but which; is our response to God's Word and works one of faithfulness, or rebellion? This answer does not simply determine whether we go to church, mosque, synagogue or temple, it affects how we view marriage and family, human society, education, law and yes, politics and government! It is productive of the differences in how we view all the critical questions of life and social order:

> Revelation throws the fire of the antithesis upon the earth. It divides parents and children; it sets friend against friend; it drives rifts within the nation; it turns humankind against

itself. "Do not think that I came to bring peace on earth," says the savior, "I have not come to bring peace, but a sword" (Matt. 10:34).[4]

## THE RISE OF SECULARISM

Although the provenance of the term *religion* implies tying and binding together, unity is not typically the first thing people tend to think of when religion is discussed in our time. In fact, the 'ties that bind' have in many ways been cut in modern culture. In the Western world, after the Reformation, and following the religious wars of the sixteenth and seventeenth centuries, a sense of religious unity in the kingdoms and empires of Christendom was increasingly ruptured at the societal level. During the Enlightenment, the notion of a supposedly *religiously neutral* secular state, built in terms of a rationalistic scientific method, was born, gradually invoking a *public-private, secular-sacred* separation of life in the name of achieving unity and tolerance for civil society and government.

That this sentiment is still with us and dominates the public discourse is evident from the Dalai Lama's recent book, *An Appeal to the World,* in which this widely celebrated 'global spiritual leader' writes in the opening paragraph, "For thousands of years, violence has been committed and justified in the name of religion…; for that reason I say that in the twenty-first century, we need a new form of ethics *beyond religion.* I am speaking of *secular* ethics."[5] He goes on to say that the basis of this new ethic is our fundamental human spirituality! The ambiguity and self-contradiction involved in this claim is obvious – how can a secular ethic grounded in human spirituality be *beyond religion* i.e. escape fundamental religious assumptions about the world?

We will examine the religious character of this secular spirituality in due course. For now it is sufficient to note that based on what we have observed about the true character of religion, it is impossible for anyone who exercises office in political and civic life to be *free from religious conviction* – both in terms of their posture toward God and in regard to what they believe is true or false concerning the aspects and structures of reality.

For example, in political life we are immediately confronted with the fundamental questions: what is the meaning of government; what is the source of governmental authority; what is the state; what is the purpose of the state; and what should be promoted and enforced as good and right in society by a just state? For the Lama, the answer to the last question is that the just state would promote 'secular ethics.' But all such ideas about justice and society are shaped by acknowledged or unacknowledged religious presuppositions – in other words by a *worldview*. To simply speak in general terms of the 'authority' or 'legal competence' of civil government immediately invokes normative states of affairs i.e. the nature of authority, legality and the ground of competency, which all require a religious worldview foundation.

In addition, the religiously-motivated move of artificially creating a strict *sacred-secular*, *private-public* divide (a dichotomy not found in real people's lives, but imposed upon them) meant that *secularism* essentially *replaced* Christianity as the new public faith of the West, the new religion of state, and the ostensible glue holding Western society together. At the same time, by affirming a *religious relativism* wherein all faiths are to be regarded and treated equally, while in the same breath declaring itself non-religious, secularism brilliantly enthroned itself as the *ultimate religious principle*.

Our culture thus invokes an abstract *dualism* that is said to separate 'faith' from the public affairs of civil government in the interest of unity, but which is in fact designed to deprivilege Christianity and thereby protect the religious assumptions of secularism from being challenged. Those assumptions are grounded in a *dogmatic belief* in the absolute autonomy and independence of human thinking. South African philosopher Danie Strauss highlights the religious motif of these political ideas at the beginning of the Enlightenment:

> The deepest motivation of the new era is found in its conviction that the human being can only proclaim its sovereignty (autonomous freedom) by exploring the possibilities of the new natural scientific understanding of reality…an *instrument* by means of which it could *control* and *subdue* all of reality. This instrument was supposed to serve the purpose of a complete *methodological breakdown* of everything within reality, introducing the creative capacities of *rational thought* to once again create *order* from this resulting *heap of chaos*… now human reason actually took over the task of creation originally assigned to God by Christianity.…Thus modern *humanism* ultimately *deified* the human being, embedded in the new motive of logical creation.[6]

Thus, flowing out of the dominant thought-forms of the Renaissance and then the Enlightenment, the Christian teaching regarding *God as the giver of law*, the *source of truth* and meaning for all of life in every aspect, has been replaced by the idea of an ever-expanding *autonomy* for human affairs – circumstances in which man himself becomes the new creator of order amidst the chaos. As a consequence, the 'secular' character of the West has been taken for granted for over sixty years.

It is nonetheless true, as we have already observed, that 'spirituality' is ubiquitous in our present society, with various pagan beliefs, occultism and Eastern religions flourishing. This does not contradict what we have said so far about the rise of secularism because they flourish, as far as Western people are concerned, *within the rubric* of the assumptions of a religious secularism. Which is to say, they thrive within a secular interpretation of the nature of reality (autonomy and religious relativism) which has opened up the space for them to be promoted, celebrated and widely practiced.

It is important to remember in this regard, that most non-Christian religion is essentially a *form of atheism* because these worldviews and ideologies do not posit an infinite, personal and relational God who is distinct from and stationed outside the cosmos, governing history. As such, Eastern religions do not present a challenge to the secular claim of radical human autonomy – indeed they simply reinforce it. The Dalai Lama, calling for a secular ethic *beyond religion* is the perfect illustration. He claims, "The key to reaching harmony, peace and justice is the sharpening of our awareness of our inner reality by, more listening, more contemplation, more meditation."[7] There is no menace to secularism here, only the comfortable reassurance that all the answers lie within man himself and his autonomous thinking.

## THE NATURE OF RELIGIOUS SECULARISM

Secularism as religious *ideology* is a complicated thing to try and define simply. It is like a great river with many tributaries feeding it. At first, the very expression 'religious secularism' might sound to some ears like an oxymoron – since secularists usually think of themselves, by definition, as 'non-religious.' However, we have seen that this is impossible. The influential atheistic thinker Friedrich Nietzsche clearly *believed* secularization was the route to *salvation.* He wrote, 'We deny God, we deny our responsibility before God, thereby we save first of all the world.'[8] Secularism is thus held out as a salvific principle.

So, let's consider first the meaning of the word *secular*. It finds its root in the Latin word 'saeculum,' a noun meaning *an age,* the Greek word being *aion*, which in English is aeon. The adjective *secular* in the history of the West is now associated with a series of *dualistic contrasts* that came about when Greco-Roman philosophical thought interacted with Christianity and in many respects was synthesized with it. The European philosopher Dirk Vollenhoven argued that much of the history of Western thought is dominated by this synthesis. In fact, Vollenhoven divided the history of Western philosophy into three periods: before the synthesis period (pagan era of antiquity till ad 50); the time of synthesis (patristic and medieval scholastic era); and modern philosophy (1450 onward) which tended to reject or denude the Christian element of the synthesis, emphasising pagan elements. This divergence was manifested in the Renaissance, which emphasized the pagan side, and the Reformation which emphasized the Christian side.[9]

Simply stated, much of Greek thought held that the cosmos consisted of two uncreated substances, eternal *form* and eternal *matter*. 'God,' an unmoved mover, was pure form, thought thinking itself. This dualistic idea eventually gave way to Plotinus' Neo-Platonism in which everything that exists emanates through gradations from an absolute undifferentiated blank unity, which he called the One. Whether beginning with an eternal duality or unity, these philosophical abstractions were expressed as eternal forms or ideas and contrasted with matter. As a result, an immortal rational soul was contrasted with body, being with becoming, the spiritual with the carnal. In other words, we are given a two-storey view of reality with an upper storey considered higher (pure), and the bottom storey viewed as lower (even evil). It follows logically that the pagan view stressed *disembodiment* as the highest level of existence, privileged intellectual contemplation over manual work or creative arts, and idealized philosopher kings. Practically, pagan culture in general viewed the material realm as subordinate to the spiritual or ideal.

The synthesis is found in a medieval Christian culture that more or less embraced this impressive Greek system construing *nature* as form and matter, while arguing that God's *grace* was required to bring nature to moral perfection and usher the human person into eternal bliss. The incompatibility of Genesis 1 and John 1 – which tell us that in the beginning a personal and relational God called into being the heavens and the earth – with the speculation of an unmoved mover and eternal matter was wrestled with by Christian thinkers but never overcome. So, the basic religious cosmology of the synthesis era consisted of two realms – *nature and grace*. The church and its spiritual authority operated in the realm of *grace*, ministering the sacraments, giving spiritual oversight, and consisted of the *sacred* vocations ruled by God's revealed Word. By contrast, the world outside the ecclesiastical sphere (nature) was *secular* and was ruled over by secular authority in terms of a stoic philosophical construct of natural law.

## REENCHANTED WITH THE ORDINARY

This dualistic view generated a variety of further contrasts. Culturally, a dichotomy was set up between the temporal affairs of the world and the spiritual affairs of the City of God. This led by extension to hierarchical distinctions between occupations and vocations belonging to the upper storey of existence (the spiritual and sacred), like clergy and monks, and those belonging to the secular world of culture and politics. Even great Christian thinkers like Augustine and later Luther tended to reinforce this kind of approach. Of course, it is legitimate to distinguish between the spheres of church and state and their jurisdiction; a non-ecclesiastical sphere of life differentiated by the emergence of an independent church was part of the contribution of Christianity in undermining the priestly claims of the

17

totalitarian politics of the pagan world. But the sacred-secular divide discussed here means far more than identifying and differentiating societal entities.

Rather, I am describing a deformed Christian worldview, deeply informed by Greek philosophy, that has played a significant role in giving us the idea of the secular as an entire domain of creation that falls outside the direct jurisdiction of Christ and His revealed Word. The upshot in the West meant the so-called sacred space of grace was steadily eaten up by the secularizing tendency of the realm of nature – coming to expression in the Renaissance. During the Reformation, however, John Calvin rejected this distinction as artificial and sought to revive the Hebraic roots of biblical faith that saw *all of life* as an integral religious whole under the living God.[10]

The Canadian philosopher Charles Taylor argues that Calvin's branch of the Reformation tended toward the disenchantment of the world by abolishing a limited sacred realm, and so helped create modern secularism by breaking down a duality that persisted throughout the Middle Ages. This analysis has some merit to the extent that many kicked against Calvin's notion that *all of life* should come directly under the Lordship of Christ and His Word, thus bringing about a counter-reaction that expanded the so-called secular realm.

But I think Taylor's conclusion that Calvin's thought fuelled the disenchantment of the world is wrong. The seeds of a radically secularizing worldview were clearly present in Greek thought, even in its Christianized, Roman Catholic form – including the power and autonomy of reason and the idea of natural law as a sufficient principle for the secular world. We will see that modern secularism is really a revived form of paganism. Calvin's reformed vision effectively resisted both the ecclesiasticizing and secularizing of life, by freeing *all of life* to serve Christ, thereby *reenchanting* the ordinary life of people in all aspects and vocations with an eternal meaning and spiritual significance. The Enlightenment and Romantic periods were both counterreactions to this biblical Calvinism.

## THE CHURCH OF THE SECULAR

Today of course, the idea of the secular no longer involves the specifics of the two-storey medieval construction of nature and grace. Instead, secularism has become an interpretation of life that regards the living God and his law-Word as non-essential and irrelevant for life and thought in the modern world. The idea that we need *grace* in light of the problem of sin is routinely thought of as the powerplay of obsolete organized religion that has inhibited man's true nature and robbed him of his freedom. Guilt becomes a psychological disorder we can be free from by transcending such obstructive religious ideas.

The idea that we have moved beyond the need for God's renewing and restorative grace in Christ has involved a process of gradually distancing the living God from the real world. With the declining power and influence of the ecclesiastical sphere in the West, due in large measure to the pagan forces unleashed during the Renaissance and Enlightenment, people increasingly began to believe in human reason as *totally independent* of God. Thus, the historian Peter Gay characterized the Enlightenment as "the rise of modern paganism."[11] Accordingly, the things we didn't like about the God of Scripture were steadily stripped away, leaving us with variations of Deism, world-soul pantheism, animistic cosmic forces, or blank atheism. It is not a coincidence that these developments coincided with the rise of pagan notions of cosmic evolution given a scientific veneer by men like Charles Darwin.

These thought currents, combined with the accomplishments of modern science and technology, not to mention social phenomena like urbanization and greater social mobility, left many believing that the personal God of Scripture, a relational and covenant-enforcing God, was unnecessary and indeed *unwelcome*. Taylor is to the point in tracing the drift: "The slide to Deism was not just the result of reason and science but reflected deep-seated moral distaste for the old religion that sees God as an *agent* in history."[12]

Clearly, the idea of an impersonal deity uninvolved in historical eventuation is much more amenable to a people increasingly thinking of themselves as autonomous. Since God previously belonged only to a sacred *upper storey* in any case – periodically interfering in temporal public affairs via the church – perhaps He could be pushed further and further out so that even the spiritual sphere of grace could be liberated from a sovereign Lord and the church itself delivered from the personal covenantal God of the Bible into a new concept of the divine. Enter the God of liberal theology, popularized by the seventeenth-century Dutch philosopher Baruch Spinoza. This god is in fact one with the world; 'God' is merely the indwelling Spirit of an impersonal cosmos. The world is just a self-contained, *immanent order*, to be understood on its own terms. Hence creation was fully separated from the Creator so that man's reason could rule in the natural, societal *and* ecclesiastical world.

In this fashion the religion of secularity is seen to be rooted in a *worldview* which embraces an impersonal mother Nature and autonomous man in a world without historical revelation. Subsequently, that world is perceived not only as impersonal, but increasingly chaotic and mysterious. This irrationalistic turn thought to arrive at a kind of 'original religion' of humanity – a perspective many contemporary secularists hold must be recovered. Taylor comments on this secular concept of an original religion that,

> If we see it everywhere covered with distorted accretions, this must be because of some degeneration in virtue or enlightenment, perhaps aided by sinister forces which profited from darkness and ignorance (often castigated as priest craft). *The differences between religions, which consist in varied such accretions are all false. We must return to the simple underlying common truth.*[13]

This is the levelling demand within today's secularism which requires all 'faiths' to submit to *becoming one,* under the benevolent supervision of the secular state. At the same time it indicates a pivot within secularism from a rationalist to an irrationalist posture.

## PAGAN SECULARITY

The initial emphasis of secular thought on a *rational* but *impersonal deterministic* order, reaching its zenith in the late eighteenth and early nineteenth centuries, thus gave way to an *irrationalistic turn* positing mystical nature and subjective experience as the key to reality. These rational and irrational polarities, which are both still with us, expose the clearly pagan roots of secularization.

Following the Greeks, the nineteenth-century Romantic movement emphasized *nature* as a mystical stream of life – a great *esoteric unity* within and without. The source of life and meaning was to be found not in rational, mathematical thought, but in *feeling and experience*. With this in view, humanistic thinkers suggested that instead of positioning man *versus* nature (reason against feeling), perhaps a higher *synthesis* and unity could be reached: a unity *with* nature! A model for this has frequently been the Greeks and their political social order. R.J. Rushdoony has observed that *the [Greek] city-state was an esoteric, mystical and divine body with a kind of androgynous wholeness, and the religion of the city state was basically a fertility cult.*[14] Interestingly, fascination with gods, goddesses, fertility cults and nature as divine were basic to the European Romantic movement.

We can see then that the varied secularising movements of the Renaissance, the Enlightenment and Romanticism shared in common an underlying hostility to biblical Christianity. They opposed the idea that man is a fallen, sinful being in need of redemption by his Maker, shared a fascination with notions of an infinite universe, impersonal nature and a philosophical chain of being and saw man as the new god of creation in the process of becoming utterly free and realising total autonomy.

Together, these thought currents gave rise to what has been called *existentialism* – the philosophic atmosphere of the modern secular West. This view frees life and society from any sense of restraint or moral authority that would stand above it. As French existentialist Jean-Paul Sartre commented, "Dostoevsky once wrote 'if God did not exist, everything would be permitted;' and that, for existentialism, is the starting point. Everything is indeed permitted if God does not exist." In a similar vein, the postmodern social theorist Michel Foucault admitted frankly, "For modern thought, no morality is possible."[15]

Ironically then, with a *personal God* removed from the scene and the universe once again regarded as churning helplessly in endless cycles like socks in the tumble-dryer, modern secular man, as Francis Schaeffer once put it, *"has become a mystic."*[16] Regarding the living God of Scripture to all intents and purposes as dead, *creational meaning* vanishing with Him, modern people want esoteric experience so that they might generate from within eccentric personal 'meanings.' Experience *as experience* is key. The hope is that this inward turn will salvage 'meaning' from the abyss to which rationalistic secular thought has consigned it. But truth, as something objectively knowable in human understanding by virtue of *creational law,* is ruled out. Inwardness and subjective experience are what count.

This existential view represents the zeitgeist of our time. As S.U. Zuidema has pointed out, *"over against the adage of the*

*Enlightenment Sapere aude (Dare to be wise) Kierkegaard puts that of Romanticism: Be free, become yourself!" and: "subjectivity is the truth."* Man's very existence now *is freedom* itself. You do not *become what you are* – as though you are something definable by virtue of creation – you only *become what you are becoming.* Human beings are therefore indefinable! One can only choose (elect) oneself by wanting to be oneself (or not). This is nothing less than a secularized doctrine of the new birth and election which lands secular man entirely in the pagan world of irrationalism. Again Zuidema explains:

> The idea of self-election places man outside the scope of God's law and beyond all lawfulness; it gives the idea of human subjectivity the sovereignty which was stolen from God. The former idea is itself a *product of secularization* and, as such, has a neo-paganistic character.[17]

The Western secular existential perspective thus leads to the conclusion of the Eastern philosopher. To answer the questions of life, the truest guide is simply inward experience – every insight comes out of new experience. Francis Schaeffer tellingly commented on these looming developments in the West several decades ago:

> What about the spread of Eastern religions and techniques within the West – things like TM, Yoga, the cults? We have moved beyond the counterculture of the sixties…; these elements from the East…are fashionable for the middle classes as well. They are everywhere…. What about the growth of

occultism, witchcraft, astrology...? people are looking for answers – answers they can experience.... Wherever we look this is what confronts us: irrational experience.[18]

## A SECULAR UTOPIA

In one sense then, we have made a great intellectual loop in the Western world. Pagan thinking has boomeranged. We began pre-Christian and thoroughly pagan. The gospel was effectively spread by the Patristic church, but Christian theology began to make room (via a synthesis) for Greek philosophical ideas as pagans were converted, eventually adopting a *dualistic view of the world* with upper and lower storeys within nature (two substances). This led to the emergence of a 'secular' realm and a series of artificial *contrasts within creation*. Subsequently, with various humanistic movements in the history of Western thought determined to recover essentially pagan Greek ideals, the Christian faith was pushed further and further back into a supposedly private, sacred, spiritual upper storey of reality, increasingly irrelevant to the real, historical world. In our time, this 'spiritual' realm is increasingly restricted to the private thoughts between your ears, not to be uttered in any cultural arena.

The result for society has been that the rapidly expanding secular domain has more or less eaten up what was left of the philosophical construction of a *sacred* domain – which for centuries managed (through the public strength of the institutional church) to influence the values of society as a whole. In so doing, secularism's impersonal worldview has opened up the public space to a recovery of numerous forms of pagan spirituality and practices that do not challenge man's radical claim to autonomy – all in the name of equality, justice, tolerance and religious *relativism*. As BJ Van Der Walt has written:

> Irrationalism taught that all religions are equally true. Pluralism no longer implies just mild but radical relativism…irrationalistic pantheism and mysticism of the late twentieth century [claims] all paths lead to god. Therefore it does not matter which road the individual selects for his spiritual journey.[19]

So, just like the ancient world, all the cults and gods are welcome, so long as they pay homage to the autonomous freedom of man. All religions (in their inner essence) are equally true, because they are different rivers running to the same sea; different roads to the same mountain peak, different paths leading back to an original spiritual religion of humanity. All human faith traditions are merely man-made, emerging from the chaos of historical development. They are culturally conditioned and therefore transient, temporary phenomena that are historically determined – they are thus *relativized*.

In our time, this reigning pagan-secular spirit even governs how we think about government. A secular, autonomous vision of man, liberated from the distasteful intrusions of a personal, sovereign God, has meant the obvious necessity of building a utopia – a *secular polis* – the kingdom of man. The presuppositions of a secular worldview require a political religion capable of absorbing mankind and all his 'faiths' into an *immanent One* – the pagan state – with its secular ethics and religion of humanity arising from within. Here unity is the supreme secular virtue, and religious division is anathema. This is why the faithful preaching of the gospel of the kingdom God is the one thing that cannot be tolerated, because it destroys man's claim to self-creation, self-election, self-definition and do-it-yourself redemption. The result for thinking about human government, as Schaeffer pointed out, is

> …gravitation toward some form of authoritarian government… and the freedoms, the sorts of freedoms we have enjoyed in the West are lost…; the growing loss of freedoms in the West are the result of a worldview which has no place for "people."[20]

Western secularism is ultimately a paradox. As Van Houten has argued, "modern society is increasingly displaying the characteristics of the oldest *religion* that has existed, namely paganism. It seeks to hide its religious character as a means of controlling the 'public' realm, creating a political religion with a totalitarian impulse."[21] Accordingly, what we as Christians face today, in what is sometimes called the 'culture wars,' is a life-and-death struggle between the Christian view of reality and the public faith of religious (pagan) secularism. This confronts us with the critical question: upon whose shoulders is the government – Christ's or the modern state's? Where does authority and sovereignty ultimately lie?

## THE INCREASE OF HIS GOVERNMENT

Before we come to a discussion of authority, it is important to highlight how the Christian must respond to the rapid advance of pagan secularism. In terms of how we speak about our culture, we need *not* say we are a post-Christian people. It is in vogue to do so, but the reality is, we cannot fully undo the profound transformation that the influence of the gospel exerted upon the West over the past two millennia. Biblical faith is deeply embedded in our language, literature, music, architecture, structures of government and social life, laws and art, and cannot simply be flushed away by contemporary intellectuals – culture is more complex than that. Most modern political theory itself in the West has been an attempt to secularize Christian theological themes, so even as Christianity is rejected, our modern pagan secularity is invariably parasitic upon it.

This means our *secular paganism* is qualitatively different from pre-Christian paganism and carries greater culpability. What we can say is that we are increasingly *non-Christian* or de-Christianizing. And we should be in no doubt about how serious a matter that is. Today's pagan secularism is probably the greatest crisis that Western Christianity has yet encountered.

Secularism's invasion of the church in the late nineteenth and early twentieth centuries in the form of *rationalistic modernism* decimated the mainline churches by requiring God's revelation to submit to man's reason. Those denominations who surrendered to modernist secularity are now on life support, closing dying churches weekly. In its irrationalist (existential and postmodern) outfit, pagan secularity is now found deep inside the walls of contemporary evangelicalism where the authority of Scripture, the doctrine of God and creation, and a scriptural view of human identity and sexuality are under serious assault. And, in the face of what appears to be the colossus of a growing neo-pagan vision of a secular statist religion, we are confronted with the grave temptation to various forms of *escapism* and to a despairing *pessimism* about the Christian gospel and our life in the world. Naturally many Christians are asking themselves, what are we to do?

The first critical thing Christians must do is resolutely reject the *relativism of pagan secularism* with its denial of the truth in Christ and his law-word for all creation. Secular *relativism* is self-refuting because it obviously has *absolute intent* – to control the whole playing field and assert its own absolute truth. We must expose secularism's self-deception and present our culture with biblical truth and a coherent scriptural worldview with clarity, grace and conviction. The scriptures affirm four critical and foundational realities that confront all people: 1. The Triune God 2. His creation 3. His redemptive purposes 4. His law-Word, which gives direction to the totality of created reality and cannot be finally overturned by man's self-creating illusions.

In this biblical view, creation *is meaning* because it is totally dependent, at all times and in every part, on the powerful Word of God which governs all things and relates each aspect of reality to every other aspect in terms of His design and purpose. As such, no 'resting point,' or final explanation for reality can be found within creation itself. In part and as a whole a dependent cosmos points us back to God as the Creator. Consequently, life is meaning-full, because creation *is meaning.*

Second, Christians must resist the inward turn that would privatize our faith. It is not sufficient to simply affirm a *personal* faith in Christ existing between one's ears. We must take an open, public and uncompromising stand with Christ and the truth of the gospel which compels us to *openly worship* (in thought, word and deed) the living God and reject all false worldviews with our heart, mind, soul and strength. This requires refusing a pietistic reaction to the direction of culture which resigns itself to the status quo. A pietistic response implicitly accepts secularism's false division of reality into public and private, secular and sacred, reason or science and faith and thereby acquiesces to a radically limited role in the world for Christ and the gospel.

To simply affirm biblical truths regarding personal salvation, regularly meet in the church building, and do professional theology is not a sufficient response to the lie seeking to alienate creation from its Maker; this is the lie undermining and threatening our culture. We must confront systematic unbelief with systematic belief, expounding and living out a *Christian world-and-life view*, grounded in the scriptures, one that unveils the beauty of the treasures of wisdom and knowledge hidden in Christ, And we must do so not simply in private, but in *every area* of our lives. Biblical faith and life in Christ are not simply a private belief, or an autobiographical comment on subjective experience; they are *the truth* in Jesus Christ declared to all men and nations which is *self-attesting* through the power of the Holy Spirit.

Third, we must reject and attack the false dualism of secularity. I have pointed out that Christianity, in the form of a nature/grace dualism, adopted elements of Greek thought, with its own secular-sacred divide; a culture which by the time of the classical Greeks held philosophic secular thought in highest esteem. I argued that from the Renaissance onward, the *secular domain* began emancipating itself from the *sacred domain*. Now, the secular not only totally dominates the sacred, but has arrogated to itself a certain sacred character. It demands the radical *privatization* of all faith except its own. By and large believers fail to see the spiritual significance of this. When people – including Christians – effectively deny that demonic spiritual powers are at work in the idea of a 'secular' worldview, by endorsing and supporting secularization in culture, they become blind to the presence of those powers.

We have seen that secularism is, in a certain sense, the unplanned child of a deformed Christianity that is now betraying its mother and must be corrected to avert disaster. The only way to overcome pagan secularism is to go right to its root and challenge the validity of a religious worldview that thinks God and His Word can be safely pushed out of the real world or corralled into the privacy of the mind alone. We can no longer settle for a synthesized culture, where Christianity is blended with secularism and we are content to live *next* to pagan secular culture rather than *reforming* it. In the spirit of the Reformation we must reject this synthesizing mentality.

The Bible recognizes no dualism in creation but only an *integral life* of love and service to God and neighbor. *All of life is religion*, not merely one narrow aspect of it. Central to our faith is the unity of God's revelation of the kingdom of God – creation, our fall into sin, our redemption in Christ by the power of the Spirit and the consummation of God's restorative purposes in the renewed creation. There are no isolated 'parts' here, one lesser than the other, no sealed domains impervious to the redemptive power of the gospel. There is no 'secular arena' with diplomatic immunity from the rule of Christ and His Word.

A failure to reject false dualisms and recover an integral scriptural world-and-life-view in our time will make the situation we are facing gravely worse than it already is because, as Zuidema points out:

> The more the church becomes ecclesiasticized, the more it will profane life outside of the church and abandon it to profanation. …This is a problem which, unless it leads man to retrace his steps in this emancipation, will irretrievably abandon us to nihilism and the destruction of every last human worth, human honor, human value and human responsibility[22]

Those are the stakes in our era. If we do not challenge this false dualism at its root, even in the church, then not only will political idols know no limits and all government be abandoned to godlessness, but the church will go down to destruction in the name of saving its hide.

Fourth, we must apply the gospel to culture in concrete ways. The rejection of pagan secularism must become *practical*. The truth of God's law-Word must be *applied* to all areas of life – from the family, to education, law, politics, business, medicine, science and arts, all for the glory of God and the good of our neighbor. Since all of life is religion, there is a Christian and scriptural way to think and live in all the diverse aspects of created reality, in terms of God's law and norms – a liturgy of life grounded in Christ's redemptive life and purpose.

To be effective in our task and calling we need *insight* into God's law-Word in Scripture and His norms, laws and ordinances in creation for every given area and discipline. We cannot be involved in business and economics as Christians without insight into God's norms and laws for economics; or agriculture without insight into God's law and norms for farming; or government without insight into God's law and norms for political life. Digging out these treasures takes effort. The pagan secularists have been hard at work in all of these fields, working out the implications of their religious view for them – marriage, sexuality and identity, economics, education, law and arts and sciences. They have indoctrinated three generations with these ideas and the result has been radical cultural change. What have we Christians been doing?

Clearly, if we are to respond effectively to pagan secularism we need to take the time to learn what it means to be faithful servants of God in these varied aspects of life. That is the excitement and thrill of the kingdom of God. We are *called to a task* and we are to do everything with all our might to the glory of God. We can only offer an attractive and coherent alternative to pagan secularism if we live out and teach a vision of God's sovereign government of all things that conforms to the Word of God.

In addition, to see this government of God manifest in the various spheres of life we must develop numerous Christian organizations and institutions: hospitals, guilds, arts initiatives, unions, charities, schools, courts of arbitration, political parties, businesses, film studios, universities, research programs, news media and journalism platforms, Internet search engines and much more. We should be deeply involved in *all the domains of life* outside the institutional church in a distinctly Christian way if we are to challenge pagan secularism. The institutional church is one important *aspect* of God's kingdom, but the Christian life is not restricted to the life of the church.

The pagan secularists carefully select, use and focus on particular *cultural gateways* to inculcate and disseminate their worldview and message. Faithful Christians need to be equally organized and focused in utilizing and developing the various organs of cultural life in distinctly Christian and biblical ways, to make known all the laws, norms and ordinances of our sovereign Lord and the redemptive life of the gospel, disseminating a Christian world-and-life view that redirects us in all these things toward true worship and service for the flourishing of life under the government of God.

We need not only Christian lawyers, but a Christian approach to law; not just Christian artists, but art rooted in a scriptural world-and-life view; not merely Christian doctors, but a Christian philosophy of medicine; not only teachers who are Christian, but a truly Christian curriculum; not just Christians in politics, but a scriptural political philosophy. In other words, we must *apply* our faith and *organize* against pagan secularism.

Finally, we must affirm that the government of Jesus Christ over all of life applies not to *some* things, but to *all* things, not only to *some* people, but to *all* people. This simply means recognizing the true jurisdiction of Christ and the gospel of the kingdom over the totality of creation. Abraham Kuyper argued powerfully:

> Religion concerns the whole of our human race. This race is the product of God's creation. It is his wonderful workmanship, his absolute possession. Therefore, the whole of mankind must be imbued with the fear of God...for not only did God create all men, not only is he for all men, but his grace also extends itself, not only as a special grace, to the elect, but also as a common grace to all mankind.... All partial religion drives the wedges of dualism into life, but...one supreme calling must impress the stamp of one-ness upon all human life, because one God upholds and preserves it, just as he created it all.[23]

If we want to breach the wall of the secular pagan lie, we must use the battering ram of a scriptural world-and-life-view that shatters all false dualisms and reclaims *all of creation* for the glory and government of God, freeing life in all its aspects to be all that Christ intends it to be. As Herman Bavinck writes:

> Spiritual life does not exclude family and social life, business and politics, art and science ... rather it is the power that enables us to faithfully fulfill our earthly calling, stamping all of life as service to God. The kingdom of God is, to be sure, like a pearl more precious than the whole world, but it is also like a leaven that leavens the entire dough. Faith isn't only the way of salvation, it also involves overcoming the world.[24]

# Authority, Sovereignty and the Heresy of Liberal Democracy

## THE QUESTION OF AUTHORITY

In the previous chapter we began by examining the nature of religion and discovered it to be both inescapable and foundational in all of life. We went on to explore the development of secularism as an all-encompassing *religious worldview* with roots deep in pagan thought. Today Western people speak of living in a secular society, with a secular government, and I pointed out that these claims are not philosophically neutral, but rest upon very specific religious ideas about the world. The choice finally was between the government of God in life, or that of autonomous man and his experience.

In deciding between these two ideas we are unavoidably confronted with the issue of *authority* – the authority of human understanding, of the state, of Scripture and of Christians as servants of the living God, living out their faith in the culture. We need to explore the significance of the question of authority and consider what it means for the way we interpret reality and how we approach political life. This question cannot be sidestepped. It confronts us all in every aspect of our lives. Whom and what will we believe, how will we live, and by what standard? Where does final authority and ultimate sovereignty reside in human affairs?

There are a variety of ways we come to know and believe, various activities by which we arrive at our convictions and acknowledge authority. One commonly cited human activity giving rise to a *certain kind* of authority is that of science. There are numerous sciences – the natural sciences, medical sciences, operational sciences, not to mention what are often referred to today as social sciences, examining things like anthropology, economics, human geography, jurisprudence, linguistics, psychology, sociology and political science. Theology is also an important science where we examine Scripture and the creeds and confessions of the church, to deepen our understanding and insight into them. When certain individuals have spent much time studying a given scientific field, reaching a certain degree of competence or accomplishment, they may establish themselves as an 'authority' in their discipline.

However, when a Christian reads the Bible to discern God's instruction for daily life, prays, or sings the Psalms to meditate on God's Word and engage in worship, it is not a *scientific* enterprise. The act of *believing* the Word of God is different from scientific *analysis* of biblical texts, for example. Moreover, when we live by the Word of God given in creation and inscripturated in the Bible, we do not *establish* its authority, but *acknowledge* it. This is because the only kind of word that the God of Scripture who created all things can speak is an infallible one (because there is nothing He does not know fully).

When we grasp the reality of the triune God, we do so in a manner analogous to the way we 'see' the truth of mathematical axioms or logical laws – the knowledge arises in an immediate way, rather than being *inferred* from other beliefs. Similarly, the truth of God's self-revelation is not *inferred* from other more basic beliefs, but rather appears to us as indubitable and as certain as any other belief we have about reality.

Nonetheless, there is a deep connection between our *believing* activity and the analytical conclusions we reach in any of these areas we now call the sciences. This connection is critical. Both historically and in terms of the structure of our thought as human beings, all our scientific or theoretical knowledge is *preceded* by a more original, *primary* knowledge. This is the everyday knowledge of experience, of practical, immediate, full and ordinary life in created reality which deepens and grows with time – it is the experience of being human in God's world.

In this everyday knowledge we encounter norms like good and evil, right and wrong, truth and falsehood, and come face to face with the laws of God for creation in every aspect of living. One does not need to be a physicist, for example, to discern a law that causes objects to fall to the ground, nor a psychologist or philosopher to recognize the reality of moral norms that give rise to a sense of guilt and shame when transgressed. We 'know' this reality regardless of whether we can formulate the law of gravity symbolically on a whiteboard or parse out various philosophical views of ethics.

The power of this primary knowledge effortlessly produces a kind of *basic trust* that is necessary for every other kind of knowledge to be established. All other forms of secondary knowledge must presuppose this basic trust – for without it there could be no science. This trust rests on a fundamental kind of *faith knowledge*, or what we might call *religious knowledge* that is inescapable to humans as created, religious beings. This knowledge can be suppressed and distorted, but it cannot be finally evaded or uprooted.

Not that certain thinkers haven't tried. The radical German philosopher Arthur Schopenhauer tried to reduce the entire cosmos, from the human person, to plants, animals, rivers and seas, to *pure will*, so that everything which appears to us in life as obvious concrete reality is in fact no more real than a dream. Yet, at the same time, Schopenhauer was religiously enraptured by music, art, humanity and the beauty of the natural world – he didn't *live* like it was a dream. His theoretical philosophical attempt to reduce reality to *mindless will* was abortive because in the end he had to reckon with the real world that his meaningful pessimistic writing, philosophical logic, love of art and nature, all presupposed as both necessary and primary.[25] After all, if human experience is really just ravenous mindless Will, why would anyone want to take the writings of one expression of that mindless Will seriously? Especially since he argued with other 'mindless Wills,' that his mindless Will was right.

In the final analysis all our knowledge is grounded in a *created reality* which, as a mystery, cannot be comprehended in its totality by human thought. This is because human thinking itself, and the scientist himself, are part of the creation they are trying to understand: a cosmos held together and fully dependent upon Christ, the Word of God. By divine revelation, we are given primary knowledge of the true *origin* of all things and the problem of sin which introduced the sense of confusion, dread, ambiguity and anxiety that persists in human life and culture – well expressed in the writing of men like Schopenhauer or the brilliant art of British figurative painter, Peter Howson.[26] Egbert Schuurman draws the important conclusion that:

> This "knowledge" and this "recognition" imply a knowledge whose content is understood by faith. With our minds we cannot get beyond this faith content, because it is itself the *foundation* of all our thinking. The knowledge that comes from a basic trust… is knowledge in the sense of ac-knowledge, it is knowledge of the heart. This knowledge which concerns the basic direction of our life is given concrete expression in our faith knowledge, in our assent and obedience to the divine revelation. This faith knowledge keeps every scientific knowledge in its limited, relative, abstract and provisional place.[27]

In every area of human thought there is the danger that people will start to believe and trust in what a given theoretical *activity of science* says, and so elevate a secondary, provisional form of knowing to the place of primary knowledge. In other words, a person's faith subtly shifts from God to man, from revelation to scientific theories, from basic trust in God's created reality and Word, to human abstractions. The sciences are valuable tools that have the capacity to deepen our understanding of a given area of life, but they cannot *displace* created reality or revelation, *remake* the world, or provide *primary* knowledge – they are a fallible and secondary instrument. Final *author*ity resides only with the *Author* of all creation, who places human beings in His creation, made in His image, and subject to His law-Word for all things. This is no less true in biology and history than in political science or theology.

## THE CONCEPT OF HERESY

This distinctly Christian foundational understanding of the relationship of the sciences (various fields of knowledge and inquiry) to belief and revelation is vitally important when considering the problem of heresy, because the heretic is one who seeks to *establish independent authority* rather than *acknowledge* it. Here, a secondary form of knowledge acquisition based in personal theorizing and revising of received and accepted Christian doctrine replaces the primary knowledge of revelation to be confessed and *believed.* The word *heresy* comes from a Greek word (*hairesis*), the essential meaning of which is a taking or *choosing for oneself.* So the heretic is one who, in their belief, confession or teaching, has placed their personal, eccentric choice or opinion above that of accepted and received authority – ultimately the authority of God and His Word.

That is why a person engaged even in the science of *theology* (a discipline with as many metaphysical pitfalls as anthropology) must take great care not to confuse their novel opinion – even if it is a thoughtful and popular opinion – with ultimate authority or primary knowledge. Which is to say, theological concepts and systems are not *identical* with Scripture. They must be weighed against Scripture and the testimony of the church down the centuries from the time of the apostles. When theologians have conflated their novel ideas with the Word of God itself – with biblical authority – the propagation of heresy is the end result.

The faith knowledge of the heart variously given with creation, manifest in Christ, inscripturated in the Bible, confirmed by the Holy Spirit and acknowledged and concretized by the confessing orthodox church down the centuries is *primary knowledge,* while theological systems and conceptual models, though vital and helpful in deepening our understanding, are *secondary* forms of scientific knowledge, provisional, and always in reform.

It is important to note in passing that the early church leaders did not 'choose,' in terms of eccentric opinion, what would be included in the canon of Scripture. Rather they simply *acknowledged* and formally *recognized* those texts which had already been received by the churches as carrying apostolic authority.[28] Heresy then, is essentially false teaching which clearly contravenes the biblical Word and orthodox deposit of faith, denying their binding authority. The early church found itself almost immediately battling heretical ideas, arising from creative theologies that sought to fuse Christianity with various forms of paganism. Several of the most important creeds of the church were the product of that battle for a faithful *reception* of legitimate authority, rooted in Christ and His Word.[29]

Obviously, without a *received authority* as the basis of orthodoxy, there can be no heresy – the concept would be meaningless! This means that in a culture which rejects, scorns, or makes light of the authority of Scripture, the orthodox creeds and confessions of the historic church, as well as church discipline, the *Christian* concept of heresy will not be tolerated. In fact, such heresy will be viewed as unimportant, irrelevant or, in the view of some apostate churches, impossible to define.

At the same time however, a new source of authority will subtly replace Scripture (and biblical confessions) within that culture – for authority never disappears but is simply *transferred*. This new authority will be taken very seriously, and a novel orthodoxy enforced with the tools of discipline adhering to that new sphere of authority – typically the state. So the basic idea of heresy is not dispensed with, rather the form of heresy is redefined.

From the Christian standpoint, all true authority begins with and resides in the *sovereign God* and His infallible Word. The Lord Jesus Christ declared, '*All authority* has been given to me in heaven and on earth' (Matt. 28:18). The apostle Paul makes the same point crystal clear:

> He demonstrated this power in the Messiah by raising Him from the dead and seating Him at His right hand in the heavens – far above every rule and authority, power and dominion, and every title given, not only in this age but also in the one to come (Eph. 1:20-21).

To be seated at the 'right hand' is a symbol of absolute and total authority. Thus the sovereignty and authority of the triune God, as creator of all things, in this age and the one to come, is a foundational *article of faith for orthodox Christianity*. It is therefore no surprise to find that the Apostles' Creed declares:

*I believe in God, the Father almighty,*
*creator of heaven and earth.*
*I believe in Jesus Christ, God's only Son, our Lord...*
*He will come to judge the living and the dead*

In a similar fashion the Nicene Creed begins:

*We believe in one God,*
*the Father, the Almighty,*
*Maker of all that is, seen and unseen.*
*We believe in one Lord, Jesus Christ,*
*the only Son of God...through Him all things were made...*

Notice that these two foundational ecumenical creeds, which summarize the basic teaching of Scripture, affirm that the triune God is *almighty* and the *creator* of all things; that Jesus Christ is *Lord and God* and the *judge* of all. In short, they affirm the absolute sovereignty and Lordship of Jesus Christ. To deny Christ this Lordship and sovereignty is therefore heretical.

## THE INFLUENCE OF HERESY

Typically, when Christians consider the subject of heresy, we think of church councils, ecclesiastical tribunals and church order – we regard the import of these matters of doctrine as essentially confined to the church institute. After all, what relevance could a person's rejection of Christ's absolute sovereign authority or atoning death for sin have in the workplace or political life, for example? Without doubt, these church-oriented considerations are vitally important for understanding and addressing heresy. The church must confront heretical teaching, refute it, and discipline members.

But what we frequently fail to recognize are the *implications* of heretical ideas and teaching as they impinge upon life *outside* the institutional church. This oversight is serious because if we ecclesiasticize the concept of heresy and regard false belief and teaching as having relevance *only* for the life of the church, we will fail to see how heretical thought profoundly affects other vitally important spheres of life – including the political. In fact, what we believe about *Christ's authority and sovereignty* actually has far-reaching implications for *political* life and thought.

In reality, there are times when heretical thinking is only clearly brought to light *outside* the ecclesiastical sphere where religion is externalized in the rest of life. Because of the tendency among Christians today to acquiesce to secularism's radical dualistic assumptions, one foundational truth about reality is thought to bear authority in the private sphere of the church institute, while a contrary commitment can hold, at the same time, for the public sphere of cultural and political life. Because of this latent dualism, it is possible for fundamental contradictions to persist without the Christian ever clearly recognizing a basic incoherence.

This means that sincere Christians within a confessing church community may believe themselves to be essentially orthodox as far as the essential tenets of the faith are concerned, while at the same time holding to a radical progressive, liberal-democratic or even Marxist view of cultural and political life for the public space – frequently without ever recognizing a basic contradiction with their confession. In short, their ecclesiasticized confession of faith has not been mediated or contextualized to cultural and political life through a scriptural worldview in a systematic, coherent way.

Consequently, on social issues, such believers will frequently suggest to fellow Christians that the state is merely a neutral apparatus to uphold a vague common good, or that things like abortion, the redefinition of marriage or euthanasia are matters of indifference. Worse, they may even suggest that these developments are a good thing for 'society out there.' In these instances, arising either from ignorance or an arrogant setting aside of Scripture, heretical views of God which deny His total sovereignty in all of life have manifested themselves in areas *outside* the church institute. In the modern church, these cultural matters are left largely unaddressed and so false and incoherent beliefs can remain quietly hidden.

This pervasive influence of heresy is inevitable. Because religious presuppositions are the point of departure for *every* area of life and thought, not just in the church or the science of theology, heresy never confines its impact or effect within the ecclesiastical sphere. As a result, well-meaning Christians who are inconsistent in their thinking and lack a comprehensive biblical worldview can unwittingly adopt views and practices in other areas of life that are rooted in heretical assumptions. In short, Christians frequently embrace and 'baptize' heretical political theologies and cultural ideologies as suitable for the life of supposedly secular society, often for want of any clearly Christian alternative, and without ever realizing they are in denial of fundamental confessional truths of Scripture and the creeds.

## WHAT IS DEMOCRACY?

Having considered the meaning and influence of *heresy*, we are now ready to turn to the concept of *democracy* and attempt to relate the two. It may initially seem somewhat shocking to identify liberal democracy as an expression of heretical ideas. Do I not believe in the consent of the people to be governed, or their legitimate role in the election of their leaders? I do. Do I wish to replace historic democratic institutions with an absolute monarchy or some dictatorial form of government? I do not. I have no desire to do away with the hard-won cultural and political freedoms bequeathed by our Christian forebears in the form of parliamentary or congressional institutions that involve responsible citizens in the election of their political leaders, whether in constitutional monarchies or other free republics.

This being the case, what is really at issue with the question of liberal democracy – the majority view of Western people today? In what sense is the contemporary view rooted in heretical ideas? Clearly, there are a variety of *forms* (or structures) of political life, even in the Western tradition. Britain has a monarchy, an established church, a House of Lords and Commons. Canada has an upper and lower house (Senate and Commons), with a viceroy for the monarchy called the Governor General. The United States has a President (executive), Congress and Senate. All have an ostensibly independent judiciary. In all these contexts the state is a *public legal institution* over a particular territory there to serve the public interest. This is the meaning of the Latin expression *res publica*. In this sense, the modern state is republican (or a republic) by definition, irrespective of the particular form it takes (constitutional monarchy or otherwise).

So I do not intend to quibble here over the varied and particular *structures* of Western political life and which form is best; my point is to address questions of basic religious *direction*. What is the basis and source of *final authority* that gives direction to any society? Where does ultimate *sovereignty* (which is another word for kingship or rule) lie? This inquiry leads inevitably to a vital question: What is the *religious root* of the contemporary idea of democracy and is it consistent with the Word of God and orthodox confessions of the church? As Armenian-American social critic Rousas Rushdoony noted, "Behind all this is the question of authority: is it from God, or from man? If God is the sovereign authority over all things, then His law-word alone can govern all things."[30] In other words, we are really reduced to three choices for political life; popular sovereignty, state sovereignty, or God's sovereignty.[31]

In a book published in 1955, Lord Percy of Newcastle argued that democracy as ideology is a "philosophy which is nothing less than a new religion." The book was called *The Heresy of Democracy: A Study in the History of Government*, and it called attention to these foundational questions. The word *democracy* itself is derived from the Greek word *demokratia* which brings together *demos*, meaning 'the people,' and *kratos*, meaning 'authority' – in popular parlance, *people power*. The basic underlying idea of radical democracy is *popular sovereignty*. So the question naturally arises, is popular sovereignty (or indeed state sovereignty) consistent with biblical truth and an orthodox doctrine of God? In a democratic order without God's ultimate sovereignty recognized, is it not the case that man's *theoretical political idea* of popular sovereignty replaces creational and biblical revelation as the basis for social order? Ideological democratic thinkers like John Dewey held that there was a basic contradiction between the popular sovereignty of man and the absolute sovereignty of God. Christianity and the family were for Dewey essentially aristocratic and anti-democratic and therefore incompatible with his vision of democracy.

To properly answer the question whether modern liberal democracy is rooted in heresy, expressed in the political sphere, it is necessary to briefly do two things. First, we need to consider the religious assumptions of the liberal democratic tradition and where it stands now. Second, we need to consider the specific claims of Christ. From the scriptural standpoint, no orthodox view of political life can negate the claims of Jesus Christ.

## THE ORIGINS OF LIBERAL DEMOCRACY

It will be important for us to deal with the qualifier 'liberal' in the expression 'liberal democracy' as we proceed. Democratic institutions are one thing, the contemporary notion of liberal democratic society is quite another. In the first place, it is important to note that it is misleading to describe Western culture as consisting of democratic *societies* or democratic *states.* This is reductionistic because society as a whole is *not* democratic. As Strauss points out:

> [T]he adjective *democratic* acquired a new life in its use as a noun, for in this case, the state itself was identified with the substantive *democracy*, and subsequently it was combined with a wide array of adjectives…*liberal* democracy…and so on. This practice loses sight of the fact that the adjective democratic has a very limited scope…; the adjective democratic has a much more modest domain of application, restricted merely to the election process as stipulated in the constitution of a just state.[32]

Likewise, most other spheres of Western society, like the family or school, are not democratic entities either – no one voted for me to be a father, and parents do not typically put decisions to their children for a vote. Neither are churches, universities or businesses democracies, but they are very much part of society. The authority of legitimate government is actually dependent upon the nature of the *office* of government; and in historically protestant lands, the idea of office-bearing and the co-determining of who will occupy those offices of government did not come about by a revolutionary social upheaval to start society over.

Over many centuries in the English-speaking world, under the influence of Christian faith and customs, an expanding degree of participation of the citizenry in their own government developed as governing authority gradually passed from the *private* sphere of kings, counts and barons, to a *public* legal sphere in a unified territory. Inherited rights and forms of political life that empowered ordinary people, not just a landed aristocracy, establishment church clerics, or hereditary monarchy emerged, as a deepening consciousness of the sovereignty of God over all people (king and commoner alike) and the value and rights of all families and individuals came to political expression.

Here, democratic principle did not mean the will of the 51% as criterion for truth and justice (a kind of direct rule by mob), but rather increased separation of powers and societal differentiation, with more and more elected representatives in civil government. In Great Britain, the Houses of Parliament (Commons and Lords – the mother of all parliaments) balanced one another, with the Bishops in the Lords acting as the moral compass of the nation under a monarchy which acknowledged and defended the Lordship of Christ and the Christian faith. After the English Revolution led by the Puritans, more and more freedoms developed for ordinary people.

Because of sin, no system of government is perfect, but over many centuries, the fundamental liberties of democratically-elected *representative government* (which for centuries did not include many groups within society) emerged in what we now call the Anglo-American tradition. Part of that tradition was the English Common Law, rooted in the scriptures, which, though *not* the product of popular vote, played a critical role in the development of constitutional life. The English philosopher Roger Scruton once remarked that the English law existed not to control the individual but to free him. Thus, free democratic institutions *in themselves* are not problematic from a Christian standpoint.[33] Clearly, however, the development of the notion of *liberal* democracy, following the Enlightenment and French Revolution, is a much thornier matter than simply affirming a particular *mode* of electing government.

Defining liberalism itself is not a straightforward task. The term has meant different things to different people. Some see liberalism as free markets, individual rights and small government, while others see it as referring to the welfare state and big government. Although John Locke is often thought of as the father of Anglo-American liberalism, the fact is he never used the term and never called himself a liberal because these concepts were not available to him at the time.[34] The term actually referred to the principles of the French Revolution where it was birthed, and for most of the nineteenth century it was seen as French doctrine. As a result, the English were suspicious and distrustful of it. For many, this *liberale* ideology was just another word for Jacobinism – and it was viewed the same way in the United States. The *Encyclopedia Americana* of 1831 explained that the new meaning of the word 'liberal' came from France.

Historian Helena Rosenblatt points out that liberalism's first theorists were the Swiss-French political thinkers, Benjamin Constant and Germaine (Madame) de Stael. Interestingly, both of them were actually suspicious of democracy. De Stael wanted 'government by the best' and Constant wanted strict property requirements for voting. They were not interested in minimizing the power of government; Constant regarded private property as a mere 'social convention' under the jurisdiction of society.[35]

But liberalism was an evolving idea and developed new strands. Soon, German thinkers gave fresh impetus to liberalism through the political economists of the later nineteenth century. Men like Wilhelm Roscher, Bruno Hildebrand, Karl Knies and their disciples attacked the idea of free markets and advocated government intervention and state welfare. These ideas were then disseminated in the English-speaking world to great effect. It was not long before notorious liberal thinker John Stuart Mill was advocating societal reform through socialism and young American intellectuals studying at German universities were joining the attack on free markets.

As the new liberalism was gradually mutating from the older revolutionary version, debates arose on what true liberalism was, and two streams of liberalism developed – one was interventionist or statist and the other was not – tributaries that continue to this day. Many liberals, not just Mill, warmly embraced socialism. Prominent liberal thinker, Leonard Trelawny Hobhouse, argued that socialism "serves to complete, rather than destroy, the leading liberal ideals."[36] The more recent descendent in the liberal genealogy is the Anglo-American development where the word *liberal* came into common use in the second decade of the twentieth century in the United States. Rosenblatt is compelling in explaining that this was due to

> Republican progressives in 1912 and Wilsonian Democrats in 1916. To them, the word meant the new, interventionist type of liberalism. Woodrow Wilson called himself 'progressive' in 1916 and 'liberal' in 1917. Although Roosevelt's New Deal would eventually come to represent liberalism of this variety, debates continued over which constituted true liberalism,

the interventionist or *laissez-faire* variety, well into the 20th century. As yet there was little, if any, talk of an Anglo-American liberal tradition with roots deep in English history. This idea was conceived as a result of the two World Wars, the rise of the Anglo-American alliance and the Cold War. The fear of fascism, Nazism and Communism caused liberalism to be reconceptualized again, this time as the 'other' of totalitarianism. It became necessary to emphasize liberalism's support for individual rights. Because of their 'statism,' France and Germany were now found to have non-existent or flawed liberal traditions. John Locke was inducted as a founding father of the Anglo-American tradition and his espousal of property rights made the core of his philosophy...; the US and Britain joined the liberal tradition late and did so by accentuating certain aspects of it and downplaying others.[37]

This latter version of liberalism is the one that is often recommended or defended today, even by Christians, as the venerable and worthy liberal tradition grounded in 'reason.' It is true that the rationalistic Enlightenment movement idealized reason – which eventually expressed itself radically and politically in the French Revolution and its aftermath, with English, Dutch, German, French and Genevan thinkers all contributing directly or indirectly to an abstract and contractarian political vision – including John Locke. The radical *liberale* of the Revolution was subsequently tamed to a degree in these later versions, mutated and broke into various streams. But is this latter revised Anglo-American version of liberalism really any closer to a Christian view of society, and isn't the older, elitist, socialist iteration once again in ascendancy?

## THE RISE OF THE NEW OLD LIBERALISM

In an illuminating article, the Jewish philosopher and political theorist Yoram Hazony defined this liberalism broadly as referring "to an Enlightenment political tradition descended from the principal political texts of rationalist political philosophers such as Hobbes, Locke, Spinoza, Rousseau, and Kant, and reprised in countless recent works of academic political theory elaborating these views."[38] Crucially, he goes on to identify three core religious axioms that undergird the new liberal-democratic thinking: 1. The availability and sufficiency of reason; 2. The (perfectly) free and (perfectly) equal individual; 3. Obligation arises from choice.

The critical concern that emerges from this analysis for Hazony is that "there is nothing in this liberal system that requires you, or even encourages you, to also adopt a commitment to God, the Bible, family or nation."[39] In fact, none of the foundational forms of *primary knowledge* discussed earlier actually give shape to the principles of *liberal* democracy of any stripe. Despite the oft-heard claim that liberal democracy is there to protect traditional belief and historic Christian institutions in a separate sphere of 'privacy,' so as to ensure no one is coerced to be a Christian or live their life in the confines of the Christian view of the traditional family, "everywhere it has gone, the liberal system has brought about the dissolution of these fundamental traditional institutions."[40]

Why is that? Hazony says the answer is not difficult to find. In essence, although liberalism claims to be a *form of government* that ensures a wide range of individual freedoms:

> ...liberalism is not a *form of government* at all. It is a system of beliefs taken to be axiomatic, from which a form of government can, supposedly, be deduced. In other words, it is a system of *dogmas*...about the nature of human beings, reason, and the sources of moral obligations that bind us...; there are no grounds for the claim that liberalism is merely a system of 'neutral' rules, a 'procedural system' that can make traditional political and religious structures work all the better while leaving them intact. Liberalism is a substantive belief system that provides an alternative foundation...[that] has not co-existed with earlier political tradition, rooted in the Bible, as we were told it would. It has rather cut this earlier tradition to ribbons.[41]

Samuel Burgess likewise notes, "Both liberalism and socialism have sought to exorcise religious belief from politics in their own way,"[42] only to replace it with their own religious confessions. The construction of an alternate belief system to Christianity to forge a new type of society is to be expected from the children of the Enlightenment and French Revolution. As Guillaume Groen van Prinsterer pointed out, "The Revolution, with its variety of schools of thought and its successive historical manifestations, is the consequence, the application, the unfolding of unbelief. The theory and practice of unbelief shaped the philosophy and the Revolution of the eighteenth century."[43]

But a very serious problem arises when the people of God, especially those who are in teaching and leadership roles in the church, downplay, ignore, or even support the dogmatic *religious* assumptions that undergird the *liberal* democratic ideal. Despite its evident anti-Christianity on display in our time, marginalizing and persecuting the faith out of the public space, Christian leaders and thinkers are frequently at pains to defend liberal democracy as a 'neutral' and purely 'procedural' system. As we will see, such a claim to neutrality is badly misguided and continues to do great damage in our culture.

Edmund Burke, one of Britain's greatest parliamentarians, a contemporary of William Wilberforce and author of *Reflections on the Revolution in France*, believed that the Christian faith was the only true basis for civil society and the source of all good and comfort – he openly challenged the emerging liberal idea of neutrality in political life. For Burke the *sovereignty of God* was the source of all delegated human power and authority.[44] He saw this biblical view of society under assault by the French *philosophes* and revolutionaries – a revolution which proved to be the mother of many subsequent political revolutions in Europe and beyond. Burgess comments that "In Burke's eyes it was not just the law of man, but the law of God that the revolutionaries were violating. If *Reflections* is concerned with a contract between the living, the dead and future generations, it is equally concerned with the contract between Heaven and Earth."[45]

The French *philosophes* denied that society is an historical-cultural development, God-given and subject to His norms and providential sovereign government. Rather, they saw it as the result of a rational *social contract* made by free and autonomous individuals. Burke recognized that, beneath the veneer of their liberal discourse concerning equality, liberty and brotherhood, the Revolutionaries were pursuing the elimination of the Christian faith from every sphere of life. The *philosophes* were radical de-Christianizers and the Revolution put their vision into action. For them political order was not something to be normed by creational law, inherited or received, but *established* by their idea of reason.

Burke understood that the hostility engendered by their cult of reason would not end with an assault on the Christian church, but rather – given the attempted destruction of the Christian faith as a whole – would also come with an assault on property, genuine liberty, and life. The sheer brutality of the Revolutionary period in the destruction of churches, civil freedoms, political opponents, property and lives in a vindictive bloodbath that ended in the Napoleonic dictatorship, bears out these concerns.

As we have seen, the French *philosophes* were picking up and extending the intellectual legacy of various Enlightenment thinkers, including elements from Locke, a child of the English Civil War – who is often burdened with the dubious honor of being a founding father of liberalism, which, as we have noted, is somewhat anachronistic.

That said, Locke's thought, which influenced both Rousseau and Voltaire, was rooted in the Enlightenment rationalistic ideal of mathematical reasoning – a thought process in which most of the sciences were effectively reduced to the *numerical* aspect of reality. That is to say, rationalistic political theorists hoped they could demonstrate that political life could likewise be reduced to a kind of mathematical demonstration. Government could surely be developed and grounded in terms of clear, rational principles. This they thought could be done in an essentially neutral fashion that would be independent of any religious commitment or historical-cultural baggage. These thinkers believed their vision was based on 'self-evident' facts, clear to all rational people. In pursuing a basic moral axiom that every 'rational' person could agree on, Locke himself provided the rudimentary building materials for the idea that all people are perfectly free, autonomous, and endowed with natural rights.

Although Locke was evidently *not* trying to develop a sweepingly secular, liberal democratic society, his thought gave inspiration to more radical thinkers because he had needlessly set aside God's creational and moral order in pursuit of the illusion of religiously neutral 'facts.' Locke was supplanting creational and biblical revelation by making man's reason, rather than the Word of God, the basis of justice and civil concord. Even the older pre-modern idea of natural law as something *external* and given was now jettisoned in favor of natural rights that emerged from man's reason.[46] Shades of the contemporary liberal democratic perspective can be detected in Locke's words:

> The state of nature has a law of nature to govern it, which obliges everyone: and *reason, which is that law,* teaches all mankind, who will but consult it, that all being equal and independent, no one ought to harm another in his life, health, liberty, or possessions.[47]

This view of the human person as essentially a rational soul, morally obliged to a law of reason, both independent and equal (in a pseudo-mathematical sense) is nowhere to be found in Scripture. In biblical faith, man is a fallen sinner. His human understanding (or reasoning) is distorted and depraved by rebellion against God, often leading him radically astray and he is anything but independent and autonomous.

## THE MYTH OF NEUTRALITY

From the Christian standpoint, man is under law in every area of life and not only is he dependent upon God and subject to Him in the totality of his being but he is set in profound mutual interdependence with other people – including those long dead who shaped the culture and customs of the society in which he lives. According to Scripture, a person's whole life is embedded in a created and covenantal reality that immediately relates us to God and then to others in mutual society from the moment of birth.[48]

People are emphatically *not* voluntary participants in a religiously neutral, self-evidently rational society, created by the contractual fiat word of abstract individuals in an idealized state of nature. Rather, all people are set in families, cultures and societies, made as image-bearers of God, having equal intrinsic value and worth, equally subject to God's law in all things and equally in need of Christ's redemptive life and work. But biblical faith nowhere says all people are perfectly free, rational and equal in the rationalistic sense, nor are they independent of pre-existing familial and social duties and obligations. As Hazony notes:

Whereas Hebrew Scripture depicts human reason as weak, capable only of local knowledge, and generally unreliable, *liberalism* depicts human reason as exceedingly powerful, offering universal knowledge, and accessible to anyone who will but consult it. Similarly, whereas the Bible depicts moral and political obligation as deriving from God and inherited by way of familial, national and religious tradition, liberalism makes no mention of either God or inherited tradition, much less specific traditional institutions such as the family or nation.[49]

Locke's faulty assumptions about the human person inescapably led to faulty assumptions about political life. Government itself can now become a *creation* of the people, beholden to the people and dissolvable by the people, for it is simply a *contract* between free, independent and equal individuals. Moreover, in keeping with these philosophical axioms, Locke wanted to neatly keep the concerns of church and state totally separate, because like the social contract in public political society, the church is just another kind of *voluntary* society occupying the private space. The affairs of religion and the affairs of the magistrate are supposedly entirely unrelated. The state (the public area), is ostensibly free of metaphysical religious claims and so in theory should leave the 'private' sphere of religion to organize and go its own way. Burgess' analysis of this naïve position is telling:

Locke consistently attempts to avoid the conclusion that in disputed cases the state may need to take its own theological character seriously…. [T]he state is not a neutral arbitrator, but necessarily has its own ethical and indeed theological values so the citizen is at times confronted with a clash of civic and religious duties.... And herein lies one of the fundamental problems faced by modern liberal democracies: they have forgotten that their own beliefs are theological in nature and not simply the product of reason. The idea of human beings as bearers of natural rights is not a theologically neutral position. The state makes judgements as to which expressions of religion are acceptable in the public sphere according to its own theological account of humans as rational, autonomous beings who are equal and bearers of natural rights.... [T] he assertion of subjective rights is incoherent without the theological roots of those rights.[50]

Locke thus failed to appreciate that a functional separation of institutions does not preclude religion occupying a central role in civil and political life. Like modern liberals, he simply overlooks the fact that his own beliefs did not emerge from an autonomous, abstract, independent reason. The idea of basic inherent rights (like property rights, conscience rights, right to a fair trial etc.), along with duties and responsibilities for all people in human society arose gradually in a Christianized culture, where human persons were viewed as God's image-bearers.

The contemporary misplaced belief that the 'truth' of liberal, egalitarian democracy is evident to all reasonable people of goodwill, because it arises from a supposedly *religiously neutral* public reason (and thus should be the basis of all valid government), ironically leads to a remarkable degree of intolerance. With the French Revolution, these assumptions produced a ferocious anger toward Christian people and churches, despite explicit legal provisions for freedom of religion! As revolutionary liberalism mutated, intolerance to Christianity has proven intractable. This leads us to a consideration of current liberal democratic thought and its claim to sponsor the human rights of all citizens over and above the promotion of any particular conception of the good.

## TODAY'S LIBERAL DEMOCRACY

Many modern liberal thinkers took up this Lockean logic, pushing it to much greater levels of abstraction, but perhaps none more notable than the American thinker John Rawls. Rawls looked to refine for the twentieth and twenty-first centuries the rationalistic and contractarian thinking of Locke, Rousseau, and Kant. Like his predecessors, Rawls begins with an idol – an abstract rational man, free and equal, possessing natural rights from which we can supposedly deduce a rational form of government. He offers no metaphysical validation for his claims about the human person; they are creedal, dogmatic statements of belief. For Rawls, man is a political animal, justice is 'fairness,' and reasonable, rational citizens will support his 'just' view of society that is based on the overlapping consensus of reasonable individuals, not theological foundations from revealed religion. Since reason is supposedly public (and neutral), arguments should be framed on those neutral terms, in a manner that everyone might agree on:

Any comprehensive doctrine, religious or secular, can be introduced into any political argument at any time, but I argue that people who do this should also present what they believe are public reasons for their argument. So their opinion is no longer just that of one particular party, but an opinion that *all members of a society might reasonably agree to*, not necessarily that they would agree to. What's important is that people give the kinds of reasons that can be understood and appraised apart from their particular comprehensive doctrines.[51]

Rawls either does not appreciate or is unwilling to acknowledge that 'reasons' cannot be properly appraised or understood outside of the comprehensive doctrines (or worldviews) from which those 'reasons' (to be comprehensible) arise, nor does he acknowledge that his own perspective on the just society is itself a comprehensive doctrine.

Christians can certainly offer reasons for their political arguments that non-Christians may well agree with, but not for the reasons Rawls thinks. Unfortunately, his confused view inevitably leads to the incoherent situation inherent in modern liberal democracies today – that there can be no public privileging of any one religion, except secular liberal democracy and its notion of public reason. This doctrine necessarily enforces the interiorization and relativization of non-secular religious belief. Christianity can have a voice only insofar as it can make common cause with Islam, Buddhism, Hinduism or paganism, and that only when it enters the discussion in terms of a public reason the secular liberal can accept.

Like Locke, Rawls seeks to banish religious belief from the sphere of government but does so by arguing for a distinction between *privately* held religious *beliefs* and common 'reason.' Beliefs that are allegedly not obvious and evident to the *common public reason* of other citizens are ruled out of bounds for political life. But as we have seen, this just begs the question: what is reasonable, fair and just, and by what standard? Moreover, who has the right to decide what are *private* beliefs and what constitutes common reason? In what sense and on what grounds are Rawls' beliefs about humanity as rational, free and equal, or his immanence perspective on justice as 'fairness,' to be regarded as *public* and the Christian view of man as God's image-bearer subject to transcendent laws of justice merely private? In reality, liberalism is a comprehensive doctrine which simply asserts itself over the Christian faith and tradition, despite being a supposedly naked political conception.

The net result is that the influence of Christianity is deliberately and severely limited by liberal democracy within its political-orthodox confession of man as a reasonable, equal being, in possession of natural rights ascertained by the reason of the sovereign common people. Yet a radically denuded, abstract concept of man as rational, atomistic, asocial, equal, free and solitary is an idol that bears no relationship to created reality and which places man, either individually or collectively, in the position of *ultimate sovereignty* – the creator of rights, authority and government in terms of his idea. Freedom for Christianity exists here only insofar as its truncated and interiorized confession leaves untouched and unchallenged the basic premises of the liberal contractarian creed. Institutions and organizations which challenge this creed today are under threat because liberal democracy must isolate and destroy the challenge to secular man's sovereignty. If possible, dissenters must be cured of their religious disease in public school. As Jonah Goldberg has pointed out:

> Beneath the individualistic rhetoric lies a mission for democratic social justice, a mission [John] Dewey himself defined as a *religion*. For other progressives, capturing children in schools was part of the larger effort to break the backbone of the nuclear family, the institution most resistant to political indoctrination.[52]

Within the contemporary liberal democratic views of both *popular and state sovereignty*, rooted in autonomous human reason, we see secularist theories in *political science* (remember the sciences are a secondary area of knowledge acquisition) taking the place of creational and biblical revelation, being fashioned into new articles of faith to underpin social order – democratic liberalism has become an impersonator of primary knowledge and a new confession of faith.

This religious confession has Christianity as its primary target. The Italian political philosopher and politician, Marcello Pera, has observed, "Since Christianity is the religion proper to Europe and the West, it is Christianity that liberalism wishes to banish to the private sphere or to oppose as an important religion and public point of reference."[53]

Today, this political faith is ubiquitous, permeating every aspect of people's lives. The Polish political philosopher,

Ryszard Legutko, writes with insight:

> What we have been observing over the last decades is an emergence of a kind of liberal-democratic general will. Whether the meaning of the term itself is identical with that used by Rousseau is of negligible significance. The fact is that we have been more and more exposed to an overwhelming liberal-democratic omnipresence, which seems independent of the will of individuals, to which they humbly submit, and which they perceive as compatible with their inmost feelings. This will permeates public and private lives, emanates from media…, expresses itself through common wisdom and persistently brazen stereotypes, through educational curricula from kindergartens to universities and through works of art. This liberal-democratic general will does not recognize geographical or political borders…. [T]he liberal-democratic general will reaches the area that Rousseau never dreamed of – language, gestures and thoughts…; this will ruthlessly imposes liberal-democratic patterns on everything and everyone…[54]

This oppressive reality brings with it the overwhelming temptation for believers to attempt a synthesis of liberal democracy with Christianity. Just as the second-century Gnostic philosopher and heretic Carpocrates sought a synthesis between Greek thought and the Christ of Scripture, the modern Christian is perpetually at risk of accommodating Christ the Lord to the pretensions of liberal-democratic reason. The Carpocratians had statues of Jesus, Pythagoras, Plato, and Aristotle together in their shrines. For them Jesus was a man of pure soul, a wonderful philosopher, and anyone had the potential to rise to His level or surpass Him. But He was not the sovereign creator, redeemer and Lord, the 'ruler of the kings of the earth' (Rev. 1:5). This Greco-Roman Jesus had a shelf-life only as long as that particular synthesis culture lasted. Once that culture collapsed, the relevance of their imaginary Gnostic Jesus disappeared with it.

In the same way, if we re-shape Jesus Christ in terms of the liberal democratic general will, reduce Him to the servant of man's political reason or relegate Him to an artificial private sphere with every other religious teacher and philosopher, our relevance, and that of the truncated gospel we preach, will disappear with an apostate society, just like the heretics of the past.

## THE CLAIMS OF CHRIST

This brings us to our concluding concern, the unequivocal claims of Jesus Christ. The imperial prerogatives of Christ are undeniable and clearly set forth in Scripture, being as plain as the doctrine of God.[55] Consider for example the references to Christ in Scripture as 'the Lord of glory' (Jas. 2:1); this was a term reserved for absolute royal power set forth in the great ancient kings and emperors who thought themselves representations of God in time. When King Herod, dressed in brilliant garments to reflect the sun, which according to Josephus were made of silver, stood in the temple and sought to claim glory for himself, he was struck down by God (Acts 12:21-24).

The ambassadorial command Christians received from the true Lord of glory in the Great Commission of Matthew 28 states and presupposes the absolute authority of Christ to possess and rule the nations (cf. Ps 2). A little later in Acts 2, blazing fire, a biblical symbol of glory, appeared over the heads of the disciples at Pentecost as they were empowered and equipped by the Holy Spirit for the task of spreading this evangel of the kingdom. The idea that this Great Commission and great empowering was intended for a purely interiorized faith or limited private 'religious sphere' as defined by a liberal or pagan state is fatuous:

> The ascendancy of the King of Glory, Jesus Christ, to all pretended kings of glory is most obvious. To suggest that Christ's realm should be controlled or licensed by pretenders is absurd and blasphemous. The modern state, through many symbols, claims to be the bearer of true glory.... The New Testament tells us that Jesus Christ is the Lord of Glory. It is thus the duty of the modern state to let Him in and to submit to Him, not to control Him.[56]

The gates of all life, including political life, must be lifted up to let Him in, or they will be broken down (Ps. 2; 24)! All spheres of human authority are conferred and derived from the triune God,[57] being subject at all times and places to the sovereign and absolute authority of Christ the Lord, in terms of His Word.[58]

This is a far cry from the popular perspective, even in the church of our era. With today's religious confession asserting a liberal-democratic general will – where man's reason and his political society is sovereign and in which morality and justice are *created* by the state (as reason incarnate), not revealed by God – we are witness to what Herman Dooyeweerd called "a strong revival of the ancient pagan conception which claimed all of life's spheres for the state, considered all morality to be state morality and was therefore not aware of the problem of the relation between individual conscience and state law."[59] There has clearly been a radical departure from our Christian moorings in acknowledgment and confession of the sovereignty of God in Jesus Christ for human society. As Abraham Kuyper observed, "Christian Europe has dethroned the One who was once its King, and the world city has become the queen under whose scepter people willingly bow down."[60]

In substance and content, these secular liberal dogmas are *heretical* in the assertion of both *popular* or *state* sovereignty and their implicit or explicit denial of human sin and fallenness, the salvation and Lordship of Jesus Christ and total sovereignty of God. The cry of eighteenth-century liberalism, '*Vox populi, vox Dei*' (the voice of the people is the voice of God), echoing down to the present and informing the thinking of our era is *heresy*, and is no less so because, as *political doctrine*, it is unlikely to get a Christian into trouble with their local presbytery, diocese or elders. The liberal account of sovereignty, uncritically adopted for the public space by so many Christians today, has a poor record of preserving freedom, justice and human dignity for persons made in God's image – just consider things like the redefinition of marriage, abortion, euthanasia, pornography, confiscatory taxation, poverty and delinquency driven by an assault on the family and new speech codes with their novel 'hate' crimes.

With all its emphasis on human autonomy, liberalism seeks to recreate society in the image of a rebellious and sinful humanity. With Edmund Burke we must be quick to remind fellow believers and our culture at large that neither monarchs, parliaments, senates nor the assembled masses, are *ultimate sovereign*. To deny total sovereignty to Jesus Christ in every area of life, like all heresy, is an act of revolution against God.

Groen Van Prinsterer, the Dutch statesman and founder of the Anti-Revolutionary Party in the Netherlands in the years following the French Revolution, issued this warning:

> In its essence, the Revolution is a single great historical fact: the invasion of the human mind by the doctrine of the *absolute sovereignty of man*, thus making him the source and centre of all truth, by substituting human reason and human will for divine revelation and divine law. The Revolution is the history of the irreligious philosophy of the past century; it is, in its origin and outworking, the doctrine that – given free reign – destroys church and state, society and family, produces disorder without ever establishing liberty or restoring moral order, and, in religion, inevitably leads its conscientious followers into atheism and despair.... For Christians of whatever church there is now a common cause. They have to maintain Christian faith and law against impiety and anarchy. But if they are to be adequate for this task, nothing less than Christian truth is required.... [T]he Gospel is, and always will be, the ultimate anti-revolutionary principle. It is the sun of justice that after

every night of error, appears over the horizon and scatters the darkness. It destroys the revolution in its root by cutting off the source of its deceptive reasoning.... [W]e must take up once more the work of the Reformation and continue in it...; the Reformation put the Christian principle – obedience out of love for God and as the servant of God – into practice, and when in every sphere it placed human authority under God's authority, it validated power by putting it back on its true foundation.... [T]he Revolution starts from the sovereignty of man; the Reformation starts from the sovereignty of God.[61]

In saying these things I do not claim that Scripture gives us a fully worked out political model to be simply read off the pages of the old and new testaments where human thought and creativity is not involved, but the Bible *does* give us a detailed perspective on reality from which, in conjunction with a careful study of creational norms manifest in historical political reality, a distinctly Christian view of political life can be developed. For example, in applying the sovereignty of God, a Christian politics will delimit all power and authority rejecting the totalitarian impulse whereby civil government swallows up the rest of society in parts-to-whole fashion. By embracing freedom in Christ and the liberty of life this brings, and by recognizing that in the kingdom God grants talents and gifts he expects to be used, invested and improved for His glory, a Christian political vision will promote free markets, with just weights and measures.

Likewise, by recognizing the reality of sin, a Christian view of government will be skeptical of all radical libertarianism and utopianism. Further, in appreciating our creaturehood and finitude, a Christian politics will seek to conserve what is good and true in cultural life and from faithfulness to the law of God, Christian political thought will commend justice (tribution) in the courts, care for the poor and oppressed and charitable welfare for the needy and downtrodden. In addition, from the apprehension of God's law-order in the entire cosmos and all spheres of life emerges a Christian political insistence on the rule of law and an ordered society with peaceful transfers of power.

While it is true that historically no single political party has had a monopoly on religious truth (for Scripture is the standard, not the so-called right or left), some political theories are clearly derived from and grounded in a biblical worldview, while others are not. Some views are built around the scaffolding of the Christian tradition, while others seek to break it down. The good news for Christians labouring in the political sphere is that because a scripturally-derived view of political life, informed by biblical prescriptions, bears fidelity to created reality, its fruit will commend itself to unbelievers on its own merits, even where people have theoretically rejected the foundations on which they are built. Mercifully, sinful man is not wholly consistent, which means that, in order to enjoy the fruit of Christian social order, even those who have rejected the faith can and will in many cases recognize the effectiveness and value of its principles.

Now, in an era of liberal-democratic heresy, we may take our stand with Carpocrates or Christ, with the sovereignty of man or with God. Only one of these has a future.

## NOTES

1   Augustine, J.G. Pilkington (trans.) *Confessions*. From Nicene and Post-Nicene Fathers, First Series, Vol. 1. Edited by Philip Schaff. (Buffalo, NY: Christian Literature Publishing Co., 1887.) Revised and edited for New Advent by Kevin Knight. http://www.newadvent.org/fathers/110101.htm.

2   Herman Dooyeweerd, *Roots of Western Culture: Pagan, Secular, and Christian Options*, ed. D.F.M. Strauss (Grand Rapids: Paideia Press, 2012), 92.

3   Dooyeweerd, *Roots*, 93

4   Dooyeweerd, *Roots*, 94

5   His Holiness the Dalai Lama, with Franz Alt, *An Appeal to the World: The Way to Peace in a Time of Division* (New York: HarperCollins, 2017), 4-5.

6   Danie Strauss, 'The Rise of the Modern (Idea of the) State,' *Politikon*, (August 2006), 33 (2), 183-195.

7   Dalai Lama, *Appeal*, 10.

8   Friedrich Nietzsche, cited in Kornelis A. Bril, *Vollenhoven's Problem-Historical Method: Introductions and Explorations* (Sioux Center, IA: Dordt College Press, 2005), 97.

9   Bril, *Vollenhoven's Problem-Historical Method*, 93-94.

10  Abraham Kuyper, *Lectures on Calvinism* (Grand Rapids: Eerdmans, 1931).

11  Peter Gay, cited in Bril, *Vollenhoven's Problem-Historical Method*, 95.

12  Charles Taylor, *A Secular Age* (Cambridge, MA: Harvard University Press, 2007), 274.

13  Taylor, *A Secular Age*, 292-293. Emphasis added.

14  R.J. Rushdoony, *The One and the Many: Studies in the Philosophy of Order and Ultimacy* (Fairfax, VA: Thoburn Press, 1971), 75.

15  Sartre and Foucault, cited in Bril, Vollenhoven's *Problem-Historical Method*, 97.

16  Francis A. Schaeffer, *The Complete Works of Francis A. Schaeffer, vol. 5: A Christian View of the West* (Wheaton, IL: Crossway, 1982) 375.

17  S. U. Zuidema, *Communication and Confrontation*, (Assen/Kampen: J.H. Kok Ltd, 1972), 154.

18  Schaeffer, *A Christian View of the West*, 378-379.

19  BJ Van Der Walt, Transforming Power: Challenging Contemporary Secular Society (Potchefstroom: Institute for Contemporary Christianity in Africa), 207.

20  Schaeffer, *A Christian View of the West*, 381.

21  Van Houten, in Van der Walt, *Transforming Power*.

22  Zuidema, *Communication and Confrontation*, 42, 48-49.

23  Kuyper, *Lectures on Calvinism*, 53-54.

24  Herman Bavinck, *The Certainty of Faith* (St. Catharines, ON: Paideia Press, 1980), 95-96.

25  Duncan Richter, 'Schopenhauer the Optimist,' in *Philosophy Now*, Issue 134, October/November 2019, Anja Publications.

26  For example, Howson's vast piece, 'The Prophecy' (2016) is an absorbing, appalling and devastating depiction fallen man's condition.

27  Egbert Schuurman, "Creation and Science: Fundamental Questions Concerning Evolutionism and Creationism," in Paul G. Schrotenboer (ed.), *The Reformed Ecumenical Synod,* Vol. VIII, No.2, August 1980.

28  For a helpful explanation of scriptural authority see James R. White, *Scripture Alone: Exploring the Bible's Accuracy, Authority and Authenticity* (Bethany House Publishers: Bloomington, MI: 2004).

29  See R. J. Rushdoony's penetrating study, *The Foundations of Social Order: Studies in the Creeds and Councils of the Early Church,* Ross House Books, 1998.

30  R.J. Rushdoony, *Roots of Reconstruction* (Vallecito, CA: Ross House Books, 1991), 25.

31 For Dutch statesman and theologian Abraham Kuyper, the normative operative principle for society under God's sovereignty was called *Sphere Sovereignty* – a model in which all spheres of power and authority were limited offices to be placed under God's absolute sovereignty. This subject is addressed in Vol 2 of this series 'For Government'

32 Strauss, 'The Rise of the Modern (Idea of the) State.'

33 For an excellent study in the emergence of political freedom in the English-speaking world see Daniel Hannan, *Inventing Freedom: How the English-Speaking Peoples Made the Modern World* (New York: Broadside, 2013).

34 Helena Rosenblatt, 'A Liberal History,' *History Today*, Vol 69, Issue 8, August 2019, Walstead Roche, 76-81.

35 Rosenblatt, 'A Liberal History,' 78.

36 Cited in Rosenblatt, 'A Liberal History,' 80.

37 Rosenblatt, 'A Liberal History,' 80-81.

38 Yoram Hazony, "Conservative Democracy: Liberal Principles have Brought us to a Dead End", *First Things*, January 2019, https://www.firstthings.com/article/2019/01/conservative-democracy.

39 Hazony, "Conservative Democracy."

40 Hazony, "Conservative Democracy."

41 Hazony, "Conservative Democracy."

42 Samuel Burgess, *The Moral Case for Conservatism* (Exeter, UK: Wilberforce Publications, 2019), 128.

43 Guillaume Groen Van Prinsterer, *Unbelief and Revolution*, trans. Harry Van Dyke (Bellingham, WA: Lexham Press, 2018), 83.

44 This point is argued extensively in an excellent new study, Samuel Burgess, *Edmund Burke's Battle with Liberalism: His Christian Philosophy and Why it Matters Today* (Exeter: Wilberforce Publications, 2017).

45  Burgess, *The Moral Case for Conservatism*, 129.

46  Burgess, *Edmund Burke*, 43-44.

47  Cited in Burgess, *Edmund Burke*, 45.

48  Cf. Gen. 1-2; Is. 24:5-6; John 1:1-13; Acts 17:23-30.

49  Hazony, "Conservative Democracy."

50  Burgess, *Edmund Burke*, 52-53.

51  John Rawls *Political Liberalism* (New York: Columbia University Press, 2005), 463.

52  Jonah Goldberg, *Liberal Fascism: The Secret History of the American Left, from Mussolini to the Politics of Change* (New York: Broadway Books, 2007), 326-327.

53  Marcello Pera, *Why We Should Call Ourselves Christians* (New York: Encounter Books, 2008), 33.

54  Ryszard Legutko, *The Demon in Democracy: Totalitarian Temptations in Free Societies* (New York: Encounter Books, 2016), 65.

55  See, as a representative sample, Psalm 2; 24; 110; John 1; 1 Cor. 15:24-26; Eph. 1; Phil. 2:9-11; Col. 1; Rev. 1:5.

56  R.J. Rushdoony, *Christianity and the State* (Vallecito, CA: Ross House Books, 1986), 73-74.

57  Cf. Prov. 8:15; Is. 40:15-17, 23-24; 49:22-23; John 19:1-11; Rom. 13:1-4; Rev. 1:5.

58  Cf. Matt. 5:17-20; 24: 35; Acts 7:55-56; Heb. 1:3; 10:12; 1 Cor. 15:24-28; Eph. 1:20-21; Col. 3:1.

59  Herman Dooyeweerd, *The Struggle for A Christian Politics: Collected Works, Series B – Volume 17* (New York: Paideia Press, 2008), 71.

60  Abraham Kuyper, *Pro Rege: Living Under Christ's Kingship: Collected Works in Public Theology, Vol 1* (Bellingham WA: Lexham Press, 2016), 72.

61  Guillaume Groen Van Prinsterer, *Christian Political Action in an Age of Revolution* (Aalten, The Netherlands: WordBridge, 2015), 8, 88-89.